Lerner SPORTS

SPORTS TEAM SMACKDOWN

CHICAGO BULLS VS. DETROIT PISTONS

RIVAL RUMBLE

JOSH ANDERSON

Lerner Publications ◆ Minneapolis

To Evie. We were watching the same Bulls game, so many miles apart, so many years before our love story began.

The stats and information in this book are accurate through the 2024–2025 NBA regular season.

Lerner Publications Company
An imprint of Lerner Publishing Group, Inc.
241 First Avenue North
Minneapolis, MN 55401 USA

For reading levels and more information, look up this title at www.lernerbooks.com.

Main body text set in Aptifer Sans LT Pro.
Typeface provided by Linotype AG.

Library of Congress Cataloging-in-Publication Data

Names: Anderson, Josh author
Title: Chicago Bulls vs. Detroit Pistons : rival rumble / Josh Anderson.
Other titles: Chicago Bulls versus Detroit Pistons
Description: Minneapolis, MN : Lerner Publications, [2026] | Series: Sports team smackdown (Lerner sports) | Includes bibliographical references and index. | Audience: Ages 7–11 | Audience: Grades 2–3 | Summary: "The Chicago Bulls and Detroit Pistons have a history of exciting matchups and heated rivalry. But which one is the best? Learn the best moments and key stats then decide for yourself!"—Provided by publisher.
Identifiers: LCCN 2025013253 (print) | LCCN 2025013254 (ebook) | ISBN 9798765689523 library binding | ISBN 9798348029388 paperback | ISBN 9798765699140 epub
Subjects: LCSH: Basketball teams—United States—Juvenile literature | Chicago Bulls (Basketball team)—Juvenile literature | Detroit Pistons (Basketball team)—Juvenile literature | Sports rivalries—United States—Juvenile literature | National Basketball Association—Juvenile literature
Classification: LCC GV885.1 .A55 2026 (print) | LCC GV885.1 (ebook) | DDC 796.323—dc23/eng/20250604

LC record available at https://lccn.loc.gov/2025013253
LC ebook record available at https://lccn.loc.gov/2025013254

Manufactured in the United States of America
1 – CG – 12/15/25

TABLE OF CONTENTS

INTRODUCTION

GRABBING THE TORCH

By 1991, many people agreed that Michael Jordan was the best player in the National Basketball Association (NBA). But Jordan and the Chicago Bulls had yet to play in the NBA Finals. In both 1989 and 1990, the Detroit Pistons beat the Bulls in the

Michael Jordan (left) reaches to block a shot from Pistons guard Joe Dumars during the 1991 playoffs.

Eastern Conference Finals. Both times, the Pistons went on to win the NBA championship.

The Pistons and Bulls faced off in the Eastern Finals for the third year in a row in 1991. The Bulls won the first three games of the series. And with under three minutes left in the first half in Game 4, the Bulls held a 49–44 lead.

Bulls All-Star forward Scottie Pippen took a jump shot that just missed. Bulls forward Horace Grant grabbed the rebound. He passed the ball to Michael Jordan.

FAST FACTS

- **The Chicago Bulls joined the NBA as an expansion team in 1966.**
- **The Pistons defeated the Bulls in the Eastern Conference Finals in 1989 and 1990.**
- **Chicago won six titles between 1991 and 1998.**
- **Detroit's 2004 NBA championship team was known for its defense.**

Jordan shot before any defender could cover him. The ball fell through the net, putting the Bulls up 51–44. The game ended in a 115–94 victory for the Bulls. It marked the end of Detroit's championship era and the beginning of the Bulls dynasty. Jordan and the Bulls would go on to win six titles from 1991 to 1998.

The Bulls and Pistons have been two of the toughest teams in the NBA's Eastern Conference. But which one is best? Let the Smackdown begin!

Jordan led the Bulls to their first NBA title in 1991.

SMACKDOWN!

CHAPTER 1

Bob Lanier (left) scored 15,488 points during his 10 seasons with the Pistons.

EASTERN CONFERENCE RIVALS

The Pistons began play in the late 1930s in Fort Wayne, Indiana. They became a professional team in 1941. The Pistons played in both the National Basketball League and the Basketball Association of America. The NBA was formed when these two leagues merged in 1949.

The Pistons reached the NBA Finals in 1955 and 1956 but lost both times. In 1957, the team moved to Detroit, Michigan.

Although they made the playoffs often, they didn't return to the Finals for more than 30 years. In the 1970s, the Pistons had one of the NBA's best players, Bob Lanier. An eight-time All-Star, Lanier was a top scorer. But his success didn't lead the team to titles.

The team's luck changed when they picked guard Isiah Thomas in the 1981 NBA Draft. Nicknamed the "Bad Boys" for their tough style of play, Thomas led this Pistons team to three straight NBA Finals from 1988 to 1990. After losing to the Los Angeles Lakers in 1988, Detroit defeated them in a 1989 rematch. The Pistons won the title again in 1990 with a win over the Portland Trail Blazers.

Isiah Thomas (right) played his entire 13-year career with the Pistons.

Years later, the Pistons found success again with a team built around star defender Ben Wallace. In 2004, they surprised many fans by defeating the Lakers in the Finals. Detroit reached the Finals again in 2005 but lost to the San Antonio Spurs.

The Bulls joined the NBA as an expansion team in 1966. Hall of Fame forward Chet Walker led the team to four

Ben Wallace holds up the NBA championship trophy after beating the Lakers in the 2004 Finals.

Michael Jordan led the University of North Carolina to a national championship in 1982. He joined the Bulls two years later.

50-win seasons from 1971 to 1974. They made it to the conference championship twice during this time but never made the Finals.

In 1984, the Bulls picked Michael Jordan in the NBA Draft. Jordan led the Bulls to three straight championships from 1991 to 1993. After briefly retiring, Jordan returned to lead another three-peat from 1996 to 1998. The Bulls set an NBA record by winning 72 games in the 1995–1996 season.

The Bulls found success again in the early 2010s. With star guard Derrick Rose, they finished with the NBA's best record in 2010–2011. That year, the Bulls reached the Eastern Conference Finals but lost to the Miami Heat.

While neither the Bulls nor the Pistons have been in the playoffs much in recent years, both teams have lots of potential. Chicago has talented young players on the roster,

Derrick Rose goes for a dunk against the Miami Heat in 2011.

Phil Jackson won two NBA titles as a player and 11 as a coach.

including Coby White and Ayo Dosunmu. Cade Cunningham is Detroit's best player. It may not be long before these rivals return to the top of the NBA.

CHECK IT OUT

Former Bulls coach Phil Jackson holds the NBA record for championships. He led the Bulls to six from 1991 to 1998, and the Los Angeles Lakers to five between 2000 and 2010.

CHAPTER 2

Dave Bing (left) avoids a block during a 1974 game against the Washington Bullets.

AMAZING MOMENTS

Chicago and Detroit met in the playoffs for the first time in 1974. Center Bob Lanier and guard Dave Bing led the Pistons. Forwards Bob Love and Chet Walker led the Bulls. The teams split the first six games.

Game 7 was close. Bing scored a basket with 28 seconds left to cut the Bulls' lead to 96–94. With three seconds left, Bing tried to pass the ball to a teammate. But Chicago's

Dennis Awtrey got his hand on the ball for the steal. Chicago won the game and the series. It marked their first-ever playoff series victory.

A 1983 game between the Pistons and the Denver Nuggets became one of the wildest in NBA history. The game went to triple-overtime, with Isiah Thomas scoring 47 points. Detroit won 186–184 in the highest-scoring game of all time. The Pistons' 186 points are still the most by a single team in one game.

Isiah Thomas led the NBA in assists in the 1983–1984 and 1984–1985 seasons.

Michael Jordan's 1987 dunk went on to become one of the most popular moments in sports history.

During the 1987 NBA Slam Dunk contest, Michael Jordan pulled off something amazing. He dribbled toward the rim, then leapt all the way from the free throw line toward the hoop. He jammed the ball into the net before landing. This feat helped him to earn one of his many nicknames: Air Jordan.

The Pistons faced the Portland Trail Blazers in the 1990 NBA Finals. The Pistons won three of the first four games. Game 5 was close. With less than a second remaining,

Detroit's Vinnie Johnson hit a jump shot to put the Pistons ahead by two. The shot earned the Pistons a 92–90 win and their second straight title.

The 1991 NBA Finals saw Michael Jordan go head-to-head with NBA legend Magic Johnson. The Bulls beat the Lakers in five games for their first title. The series was highlighted by Jordan's iconic move in Game 2. Driving to the hoop, Jordan rose to dunk the ball with his right hand. In midair, he switched the ball to his left hand for a layup. The move showed Jordan's skill and cleverness.

Michael Jordan (left) guards Magic Johnson closely during the 1991 NBA Finals.

Michael Jordan and Phil Jackson celebrate after winning their sixth NBA title together in 1998.

Game 6 of the 1998 NBA Finals ended with one of the most famous shots in history. The Bulls trailed the Utah Jazz 86–85 with under 20 seconds left. Jordan stole the ball from Karl Malone. Then, guarded by the Jazz's Bryon Russell, he drove right and then suddenly stopped. Russell slipped and fell, leaving Jordan wide open. Jordan sank a jump shot with 5.2 seconds left. The Bulls won 87–86, securing the sixth and last title of their dynasty.

Behind star Ben Wallace, the 2003–2004 Pistons allowed their opponents to score only 84.26 points per game. That was tied for best in the NBA that season. In Game 3 of the

2004 Finals, they held the Lakers to only 68 points. Wallace was named Defensive Player of the Year (DPOY) in 2002, 2003, 2005, and 2006. His 2006 award tied him for the most DPOY awards in history.

Ben Wallace (left) and Lakers forward Luke Walton compete for a rebound in 2004.

CHECK IT OUT

The Pistons selected Cade Cunningham with the first overall pick in the 2021 NBA Draft.

CHAPTER 3

Isiah Thomas dribbles to the basket during a 1988 game.

TOP PLAYERS

Hall of Fame player Isiah Thomas played for the Pistons from 1981 to 1994. He was an All-Star in 12 of his 13 seasons and led Detroit to two NBA titles. Widely considered one of the greatest point guards in history, he ranks 10th all-time in assists with 9,061 and 18th in steals with 1,861.

Michael Jordan is often considered the greatest player in NBA history. His talent changed the game. His 30.1 points scored per game is still the highest in NBA history. Jordan won a record six Finals MVP awards. He led the Bulls to six championships and never lost a Finals series.

Michael Jordan led the NBA in total points scored in 11 of his 13 seasons with the Bulls.

Scottie Pippen stole the ball 1,792 times during 12 seasons with the Bulls. He led the NBA with 232 steals in 1994–1995.

Jordan had the fortune of playing with another legend, Scottie Pippen. Pippen was a key part of all six Bulls championship teams in the 1990s. He took seven trips to the All-Star Game. He is known for his ability on both offense and defense. He made the NBA's All-Defensive Team 10 times and ranks eighth all-time in steals with 2,307.

Grant Hill was a star at Duke University before the Pistons picked him third in the 1994 NBA Draft. He played six seasons in Detroit, with 19.9 points, 6.4 rebounds, and five assists per game as a rookie. Hill won the 1995 Rookie of the Year award and was named an All-Star five times as a Piston.

Grant Hill avoids multiple defenders to score against the New York Knicks in 1996.

Like Hill, Derrick Rose won Rookie of the Year and quickly became a star. He played seven seasons for the Bulls and won the 2011 NBA MVP award, with 25 points and 7.7 assists per game that year. Rose also led Chicago to the Eastern Conference Finals in 2011.

The Bulls picked Derrick Rose first overall in the 2008 NBA Draft.

Artis Gilmore averaged 20.1 points per game during his six seasons with the Bulls.

Cade Cunningham brought new life to Detroit basketball after joining the Pistons. Detroit picked him first overall in the 2021 NBA Draft. Cunningham earned All-Rookie honors after an impressive first season. In 2024–2025, he scored more than 26 points per game and made his first All-Star appearance.

CHECK IT OUT

Bulls center Artis Gilmore led the NBA in shooting percentage for four seasons in a row between 1980 and 1984.

CHAPTER 4

Cade Cunningham drives against two Bulls defenders during a 2024 game.

CHOOSE YOUR CHAMPION

Now that we've learned more about the Bulls and the Pistons, which team comes out on top? There's no such thing as a right or wrong answer. Different people will have different opinions.

The Bulls have appeared in the playoffs 36 times in 59 seasons. The Pistons have made the playoffs 43 times in 77 seasons. The Bulls have made the Finals six times and won all six. The Pistons have played in the Finals seven times, and they've won three championships.

The teams have matched up in the regular season 285 times. The Bulls have won 147 times. The Pistons have won 138. The teams have faced off in six playoff series with the Pistons winning four.

This smackdown between two of the Eastern Conference's top teams comes down to one small edge. During their greatest era in the late 1980s and early 1990s, the Pistons reached three NBA Finals and won two. The Bulls won six titles between 1991 and 1998. This eight-year period is one of the most successful in NBA history. This amazing run of success gives the Bulls the very slight victory over their rivals in this extremely close smackdown.

What do you think? Did we get it right? Think about why or why not!

Chicago's Tre Jones dribbles past two Detroit defenders during a 2025 game.

SMACKDOWN TIMELINE

CHICAGO BULLS

1966 The Chicago Bulls begin play as an NBA expansion team.

1971 Jerry Sloan, Chet Walker, and Bob Love lead the Bulls to their first 50-win season, establishing the team as a rising force in the league.

1984 The Bulls select Michael Jordan in the NBA Draft.

1989 Under coach Phil Jackson, the Bulls begin using the "Triangle Offense," setting the stage for their success in the 1990s.

1991 The Bulls win their first NBA championship, defeating the Los Angeles Lakers.

1994 Following Michael Jordan's first retirement, the Bulls remain competitive and reach the Eastern Conference Semifinals.

1996 The Bulls set an NBA record by finishing 72–10 in the regular season.

2011 Derrick Rose becomes the youngest MVP in NBA history.

DETROIT PISTONS

1941 The Pistons begin play as a professional team in Fort Wayne, Indiana.

1957 The Pistons move to Detroit, Michigan.

1974 The Pistons make a deep playoff run, led by Bob Lanier and Dave Bing. They fall to the Chicago Bulls in a hard-fought Game 7.

1981 The team picks Isiah Thomas in the NBA Draft.

1989 Under coach Chuck Daly, the Pistons develop a physical, defense-first identity and win their first of back-to-back NBA titles.

2004 The Pistons shock the NBA by beating the heavily favored Los Angeles Lakers in the Finals to win their third championship.

2021 The team picks Cade Cunningham in the NBA Draft.

2025 The Pistons improve on the previous year's win total before the All-Star Game and earn a spot in the playoffs.

GLOSSARY

All-Star: a player chosen as one of the best in the league to compete in a game against other top players

assist: a pass that leads directly to a basket

draft: when teams take turns picking new players

dynasty: a team that is very successful for a long period of time

expansion team: a new team that is added to the league

Hall of Fame: a museum in Springfield, Illinois, that honors the best players in basketball history

NBA Finals: a series of games to decide each year's NBA champion

playoffs: games after the season to decide who will play in the NBA Finals

rival: a team or player competing against another for dominance in the same area

rookie: a first-year player

steal: when a player takes the ball from an opponent

three-peat: winning three championships in a row

LEARN MORE

Britannica Kids: Detroit Pistons
https://kids.britannica.com/students/article/Detroit-Pistons/570892

Britannica Kids: National Basketball Association (NBA)
https://kids.britannica.com/students/article/National-Basketball-Association-NBA/624441

Bulcao, Denny Jr. *Detroit Pistons*. Creative Education, 2025.

Greenberg, Keith Elliot. *LeBron James vs. Michael Jordan: Who Would Win?* Lerner Publications, 2024.

Kiddle: Chicago Bulls Facts for Kids
https://kids.kiddle.co/Chicago_Bulls

Tischler, Joe. *Chicago Bulls*. Creative Education, 2025.

INDEX

PHOTO ACKNOWLEDGMENTS

Image credits: Focus on Sport/Getty Images, p. 4; John Swart/AP Photo/Getty Images, p. 6; Nic Antaya/Getty Images; Melissa Tamez/Icon Sportswire/Getty Images, p. 7; Focus on Sport/Getty Images, p. 8; Allsport/Hulton Archive/Getty Images, p. 9; Tom Pidgeon/Getty Images, p. 10; Tom Berg/Wire Image/Getty Images, p. 11; Mike Ehrmann/Getty Images, p. 12; VINCENT LAFORET/AFP/Getty Images, p. 13; Focus on Sport/Getty Images, p. 14; Focus on Sport/Getty Images, p. 15; Bettmann/Getty Images, p. 16; Al Seib/Los Angeles Times/Getty Images, p. 17; JEFF HAYNES/AFP/Getty Images, p. 18; Jed Jacobsohn/Getty Images, p. 19; Focus on Sport/Getty Images, p. 20; Mike Powell/Allsport/Getty Images, p. 21; Focus on Sport/Getty Images, p. 22; Nathaniel S. Butler/NBAE/Getty Images, p. 23; Jonathan Ferrey/Getty Images, p. 24; Focus on Sport/Getty Images, p. 25; Gregory Shamus/Getty Images, p. 26; Luke Hales/Getty Images, p. 27.

Cover: Melissa Tamez/Icon Sportswire/Newscom; Melissa Tamez/Icon Sportswire/Newscom.